The Edible Se

Pacific Shores Cookbook & Guide

Rick M. Harbo

Barbecued oysters.

hancock

house

Cataloging in Publication Data

Harbo, Rick M., 1949-
The Edible Seashore

Includes index.
ISBN 0-88839-199-4

1. Cookery (Seafood). 2. Seafood - Pacific Coast (North America). I.
Title.

TX747.H37 1988   641.6'9   C87-091145-7

Designed and Edited
by Herb Bryce
Type is Palatino, produced on Apple computer
at Fiero Publishing, White Rock, B.C.
Printed in Hong Kong.

Published simultaneously in Canada and the United States by

HANCOCK HOUSE PUBLISHERS LTD.
19313 Zero Ave., Surrey, B.C. V3S 5J9
HANCOCK HOUSE PUBLISHERS
1431 Harrison Ave., Blaine, WA 98230

Table of contents

Acknowledgment

I thank my wife, Heather, who assisted in the preparation of many of the meals. She provided numerous useful suggestions and spent many hours proofing the drafts of the book.

Photographic Credits
FRONT COVER: Red Abalone, Steve Rosenberg
INSIDE: p. 25, Razor Clams, N. Bourne;
         p. 38, Squid, B. Hillaby; p. 55, Kombu, M. Coon.

Introduction

First, chill the white wine.

This book is intended as a field guide for the harvest and preparation of seafood by boaters, divers, or beachcombers from Alaska to California. Photographs and descriptions are given to identify common edible marine animals and plants in this region.

Many tips are given for the collection and preparation of the seafoods, as well as recipes. Guidelines are given for live, fresh, and frozen storage procedures as well as reference to basic herbs and spices to complement finfish and shellfish.

Most of the recipes are very simple and basic, to enhance the flavor of the seafood. Be innovative and improvise with what you have available. Many of the recipes are ideal for cooking on the beach or on your boat. Please keep in mind conservation of marinelife. Take only what you can prepare and eat—and enjoy.

I have not included many common seashore animals such as snails, limpets, and chitons. Although edible, they require numerous animals for a serving and are usually tough and not very tasty.

I welcome comments, suggestions, and recipes for future editions of this guide. Please write to me, care of the publisher.

Fish for good health

The average North American eats only 7 kg (15 ½ lb.) of fish each year compared to 65 kg (143 lb.) of red meat. Fish and shellfish have great nutritional value as a source of low-calorie protein, minerals, vitamins, and oils with low levels of cholesterol. Researchers suggest that eating fish can change blood chemistry, lower blood pressure, and reduce the risks of heart disease.

Fish and shellfish contain: (a) protein, (b) fats, (c) minerals, and (d) vitamins:

(a) protein: cod and sole contain 15 to 20% protein, the same proportions as in meat and poultry. Fish is never tough; there is only 3% connective tissue in fish muscle compared to 13 in meat muscle.

(b) fats: the easily digested or polyunsaturated fats are low in cholesterol and may reduce the risk of heart disease. Fatty fish, crab, lobster, and shrimp do contain higher levels of cholesterol and should be limited if you need to reduce your intake. Most fish are lean (average 2% fat), such as halibut and sole, and salmon, though higher in fats, is still lower in calories than is lean meat.

(c) minerals: a good source of magnesium, phosphorus, iodine, potassium, iron, copper, selenium, and fluorine. Calcium content is high in oysters, clams (no, you don't have to eat the shells!), shrimp, and the soft bones of canned fish, which are edible. Oysters are rich in zinc. Fish are generally low in sodium, but avoid smoked fish or salt cod if you are concerned about salt content.

(d) vitamins: the vitamin content of most fish is comparable to meat. Fish are generally a good source of B complex vitamins; fish liver is high in vitamins A and D.

Increase your fish and seafood intake for good health but also be aware of the hazards. Fish and shellfish should not be harvested from polluted waters; they may contain toxin. If you are in doubt about the safety of fish in any area, consult the local or regional fisheries office.

Fisheries Regulations—Licensing Information

Fisheries regulations include licensing information, gear restrictions, daily bag limits, possession limits, procedures for recording your catch, export limits, seasonal and area closures, public tideland recreation areas, and other prohibitions.

Fishing guides often include identification of common species, tips on fishing techniques and on cleaning and preparing your catch. Areas closed due to contamination of shellfish are listed but there are often periodic local closures that are indicated by signs or posted notices (see the following section on shellfish edibility). In the United States, contact local health authorities—county health officers—to determine if shellfish are safe to eat.

For further information, sport-fishing guides, and a list of local field or patrol offices:

1. **Alaska:** contact local field offices, or:
>   Alaska Department of Fish and Game,
>   333 Raspberry Road,
>   Anchorage, AL 99518

2. **British Columbia:** contact local offices of the federal department of fisheries and oceans, or:
>   Ombudsman, Recreational Fisheries,
>   Department of Fisheries and Oceans,
>   555 West Hastings Street,
>   Vancouver, B.C. V6B 5G3

3. **California:** contact local field offices, or:
>   Department of Fish and Game,
>   1416 - 9th Street,
>   Sacramento, CA 95814

4. **Oregon:** contact local field offices, or:
>   Department of Fish and Wildlife,
>   PO Box 3503,
>   Portland, OR 97208

5. **Washington:** contact local field offices, or:
>   Washington State Department of Fisheries,
>   115 General Administration Bldg.,
>   Olympia, WA 98504

Shellfish edibility and contamination
Bivalve Mollusks

Shellfish that are affected by sewage (bacterial) contamination and "paralytic shellfish poisoning" (PSP) are almost exclusively the bivalve mollusks. They are shellfish with two shells, such as clams, oysters, mussels, and scallops that collect their food by filtering particles out of the water. Other shellfish such as snails, abalone, shrimps, prawns, crabs, and finfish are not included in these closures.

Safety guidelines and procedures

* check with a local fishery officer for an update on the safety of beaches in the area you plan to visit.

* refer to sport-fishing guides that list permanent and seasonal area closures.
* do not harvest from areas susceptible to sewage contamination from   urban or agricultural upland uses.
* do not harvest in the vicinity of major boat anchorages.
* do not eat raw shellfish unless you are convinced that the shellfish   have been taken from clean waters.
* Do not rinse cooked shellfish or other foods in contaminated water.

Paralytic shellfish poisoning (PSP)

Paralytic shellfish poisoning, or PSP, is a form of food poisoning that results from toxic compounds produced by certain plankton. These plankton are accumulated by filter-feeding bivalves and affect humans that consume the shellfish. The toxins do not harm the shellfish.

Symptoms of PSP: The poison affects the transmission of nerve impulses. The symptoms are tingling sensations in the lips and tongue, followed by numbness and similar sensations in the fingertips and toes, and, finally, a loss of muscle control.

Outbreaks of PSP have been associated with mussels, clams, oysters, and pink and spiny scallops. Abalone, shrimp, and finfishes do not feed on toxic plankton.

PSP can occur at all times of the year, but the highest risk periods are over the summer months. Many areas are closed permanently because of the regular recurrences of PSP outbreaks and the difficulties of monitoring beaches to minimize the possibility of contaminated shellfish.

The source of PSP on the Pacific coast from Alaska to California is a microscopic marine organism (a dinoflagellate), called *Protogonyaulax catenella*.

Protogonyaulax blooms in such numbers that it discolors the water, hence "red tide." Bivalves, which filter large volumes of water, concentrate the organism and its toxins. The period of danger varies, according to the shellfish species. Mussels concentrate and eliminate the toxins very quickly, while butter clams may retain PSP for a year or more.

It should be noted that the presence of a red tide is a warning that the bivalves may be poisonous; however, the absence of a red tide does not mean they are safe to eat. To add to the confusion, most red tides are harmless, being caused by plankton other than *Protogonyaulax*.

The harvest of commercial shellfish is carefully controlled and monitored extensively to ensure safety to the consumer. All bivalves must be delivered to a registered shellfish plant and be subjected to inspection and monitoring programs.

Sewage contamination

Bivalve shellfish filter large quantities of water to gather food and can accumulate sewage bacteria from the waters in which they grow. As cautioned previously, do not harvest from areas that may be contaminated by urban or agricultural runoff. Beaches fronting land developed for residential, industrial, or agricultural use should be considered as potentially contaminated. Do not harvest near any wharf or harbor where significant boating activities occur or in the vicinity of anchorages where untreated domestic wastes are usually discharged overboard.

Shellfish from polluted waters may contain toxins, and organisms that can cause cholera, gastroenteritis, and hepatitis. Obey posted warnings; they are there to protect your health.

Handling and Storage

Procedures for live, fresh, and frozen seafood

Live storage: Low temperature and a minimum storage time are the keys to high quality. Eat your catch as soon as possible for the tastiest results. Seafoods must be chilled to prevent bacterial growth and spoilage. All products should be stored in the refrigerator below 5°C or 40°F, preferably at 1° to 2° C or 34° to 36°F. Do not store live shellfish directly on ice in a cooler.

Frozen Storage: Freeze only fresh catches. Package individual or family portions. Remove air from each package. All products should be kept frozen below -18°C or 0°F; store in the coldest part of the freezer. Label and date packages.

Thawing frozen seafood: Do not thaw at room temperature. Do not refreeze fish or shellfish that has been thawed. Do not thaw seafood that is for steaming, oven steaming, poaching, or barbecuing in foil. Thaw by placing the unopened package in the refrigerator overnight or by immersing in cold water for 1 to 2 hours. Thawing can also be done in a microwave oven using the defrost cycle. Use thawed seafood as soon as possible after thawing. It can be cooked, then packaged and refrozen for a short period.

Shellfish

Mollusks

Abalone

Live storage: Abalone can be stored in a container, in the refrigerator, covered with a wet cloth. If you wish to eat abs immediately, they will have to be sliced and pounded to tenderize the meat. It is best to refrigerate the abalone overnight so that the muscle relaxes before preparation. Freezing will also tenderize the meat.

Frozen storage: Clean and slice the meat into steaks. Wash the pieces in brine (1 Tbsp. or 15 mL salt for each qt. or 1 liter of water). Drain and package in freezer bags. Exclude air, seal tightly, label, and freeze for up to 3 months.

Clams: Hardshell clams, steamers, razor clams

Live storage: Live clams in the shell can be stored covered with a wet cloth in the refrigerator for 1 to 2 days. Make sure that the clams are alive and the shells are closed before cooking. If gaping, the clams should respond if they are alive, closing when poked gently. Do not store directly on ice or in fresh water. Discard any dead clams.

Frozen storage: Hardshell clams can be frozen live, in the shell. Freeze only if they are very fresh and tightly closed. Freeze cooked and shucked clams in a freezer container, covering them with strained clam liquor. Put the lid on securely, label, and freeze for up to 3 months.

9

Digging for razor clams

Geoducks and horse clams

Live storage: As for other clams. The clams should contract or respond to a gentle poke if they are alive. Discard any dead clams.

Frozen storage: Do not freeze in the shell. Shuck and clean meats before freezing. Wash in brine (1 Tbsp. or 15 mL salt for each qt. or 1 liter of water), drain and package in plastic freezer bags. Exclude all air, seal tightly, label, and freeze up to 2 months.

Oysters

Live storage: Live oysters in the shell can be stored, covered with a wet cloth, in the refrigerator for 1 to 2 weeks. Do not store directly on ice or in fresh water. Before cooking, make sure that the shells are tightly closed, indicating that the oysters are alive. Shucked oysters can be stored in strained liquor, in a tightly sealed container in the refrigerator for up to 10 days.

Frozen storage: Do not freeze in the shell. Freeze shucked and washed oysters, covered with strained liquor, allowing a headspace, in a freezer container. Put the lid on securely, label, and freeze for up to 3 months.

Mussels

Live storage: Mussels should be used as soon as possible after you harvest them. They can be refrigerated in a container covered with a wet cloth, but do not hold longer than 1 to 2 days.

Frozen storage: Mussels can be frozen in the shell. Cooked mussels can be frozen in strained liquid in a tightly sealed freezer container. Label and freeze for up to 3 months.

Scallops

Live storage: Cleaned scallop meats can be stored in a tightly sealed container, refrigerated no longer than 2 days. The small pink and spiny scallops can be stored, live in the shell, covered with a wet cloth, for a day. Discard any scallops that will not close tightly when poked gently.

Frozen storage: Do not freeze in the shell. Wash cleaned meats in brine (1 Tbsp. or 15 mL salt in a qt. or 1 liter of water). Drain and package in freezer bags. Exclude air and seal tightly, label, and freeze for up to 3 months.

Squid

Fresh storage: Fresh-cleaned squid can be stored in a tightly covered container or wrapped in leak-proof paper in the refrigerator for 1 to 2 days only.

Frozen storage: Fresh squid, cleaned, can be packed in a plastic freezer bag. Exclude air, seal tightly, label, and freeze for up to 2 months.

Crustaceans

Crabs: Dungeness and red rock crabs

Live storage: Dead crabs, even if fresh, should be discarded. Live crabs can be covered with a damp cloth in a container and stored in the refrigerator for up to 12 hours.

Frozen storage: Freeze cooked whole crab in a plastic freezer bag. Exclude air, seal tightly, label, and freeze for up to 2 months. Freeze cooked crab meat in freezer containers, with enough cold brine to cover meat (2 Tbsp. or 30 mL of salt for each qt. or 1 liter of water—stir well to dissolve salt). Allow $1/2$ in. headspace. Seal securely, label, and freeze in upright position for up to 2 months.

Shrimp and prawns

Live (and fresh) storage: Refrigerate raw or cooked shrimp in a covered container for up to 2 days.

Frozen storage: Take uncooked shrimp tails or cooked shrimp, wash in brine (1 Tbsp. or 15 mL of salt for each qt. or 1 liter of water), and drain. Freeze in plastic freezer bags for up to 3 months. Exclude air, seal tightly, label, and freeze. Whole, uncooked shrimp can be frozen in brine and stored for up to a year. Wash in brine as above. Pack in a freezer container, allowing for a headspace of $1/2$ in. Fill with brine solution: 2 Tbsp. or 30 mL of salt for each qt. or 1 liter of water. Stir well to dissolve salt. Store upright.

Goose barnacles

Live storage: Goose barnacles can be stored whole, in the refrigerator, covered with a wet cloth for only 1 or 2 days.

Frozen storage: Goose barnacles can be frozen whole but this is not recommended. The cooked and cleaned meats can be frozen in brine in freezer containers as described above for crab and shrimp meat.

Echinoderms

Sea urchins

Fresh storage: Clean and wash roe in brine. Drain, and store in a sealed container in the refrigerator for 1 to 2 days only.

Frozen storage: Do not freeze the roe. Prepared spreads or dips with sea urchin roe can be frozen and stored for up to 2 months.

Sea cucumbers

Fresh storage: Wash and clean muscle strips. Store in a sealed container in the refrigerator for 1 to 2 days.

Frozen storage: Wash muscle strips in brine, drain. Package in plastic freezer bags, exclude air, seal tightly, label, and freeze for up to 2 months.

SHELLFISH

Mollusks

Hardshell clams (steamers), cockles

Native littleneck clam *Protothaca staminea*:
Aleutian Is., AL, to southern California. Medium size, shell length to 2 ³/4 in. (7 cm).
Oval shells with concentric and radiating sculpture. Color is a uniform pale brown,
often with dark brown, angular patterns. Short fused siphons. Found buried one to 3
in. (3 to 8 cm) in firm beach of gravel, sand, and mud. Occurs at the mid-intertidal zone
(3-ft. or one-meter tidal height and less), and subtidally.

Manila (Japanese littleneck) clam *Tapes philippinarum*:
Central B.C. coast to California. Medium size, shell length to 2 ¹/3 in. (6 cm).
Introduced from Japan. Oblong shells, radial ribs more prominent than concentric.
Interior of the shell has purple patches. Split siphons. Found buried one to 3 in. (3 to
8 cm) in muddy gravel, usually higher up on the beach than native littlenecks.

Butter clam *Saxidomus giganteus:*
Aleutian Is., AL, to California. Large size, shells to 5 in. (13 cm) long. Thick heavy shells with fine concentric ridges. Found buried 10 to 14 in. (25 to 35 cm) in sand, broken shell, or gravel beaches, generally protected. Occurs at low-intertidal zone (tidal heights of 2 ft. (0.6 m) and less) to depths of 11 to 12 ft. (30 m).

Heart cockle (basket, Nuttall's cockle) *Clinocardium nuttallii:*
Alaska to central California. Medium size, shell length to 3 in. (8 cm). Heavy shells with 34 to 38 squarish, radiating ribs. Common but not numerous. Found on or buried just under the surface of sand, mud, or eelgrass areas in quiet bays. Occurs at mid-tide range to depths of 656 ft. (200 m).

Collection of hardshell clams

Referring to tide tables is a must for clam diggers. Tidal heights are listed in daily newspapers, or annual tables which can be bought at sporting goods stores.

Manila clams occur high up on the beach, at tidal heights of approximately 8 ft. (2.4 m) or less, native littlenecks in the mid-intertidal zone at tidal heights of 5 ft. (1.5 m) or less, and butter clams on the lower third of the intertidal zone, at 3 ft. (one m) or less where the maximum tidal range is 15 ft. (4.5 m).

Manila and littleneck clams are both found on protected mud-gravel beaches where they are buried only inches below the surface. Using a short-tined garden rake will result in less breakage than using a fork or shovel. A garden fork is normally used for butter clams, which may be buried to 12 in. (30 cm) below the surface in sand, broken shells, and small gravel.

Cockles are not buried deeply, and often sit on the surface of sand-mud flats and eelgrass beds. They can be taken by hand.

Preparation of hardshell clams

Littleneck, manila clams, and cockles: Check that the clam shells are tightly closed. This means that the clams are alive and healthy. Discard any broken or open clams that do not close when the inside is poked. Scrub the shells, and soak the clams in salted water (1 $^1/2$ Tbsp. or 25 mL salt to 4 cups or 1 liter of tap water), for 30 minutes to an hour, changing the water every 10 to 15 minutes.

Butter clams: Some discard the neck (siphon) where PSP is known to concentrate, in addition to the gills, the dark brown mass of the gut, and the digestive gland—leaving the two round adductor muscles that hold the clam together, the body, and two pieces of the frilly mantle. These are chopped or ground and used in chowders.

Cooking of hardshell clams

Clams on the barbecue

After scrubbing and soaking, place clams on the barbecue grill, 3 to 4 in. (7 to 10 cm) over hot coals, until the shells open: 5 to 10 minutes. Dip meats in lemon butter.

Steamed clams

Place clams in a steamer or sieve over rapidly boiling water. Cover tightly and steam until the shells open, 5 to 10 minutes. Strain and save the water-clam broth for other recipes. (You can freeze it.) Dip the clams in melted butter with squeezed lemon. Discard any clams that do not open.

Boiled clams

Place clams in a large pot and just cover them with cold water (or part wine). Bring to a boil and simmer gently until the shells open, about 10 minutes. Strain and save the broth for chowders or other recipes. Discard any clams that do not open.

Clam chowders

There is endless and often heated debate over the merits of New England (white) and Manhattan (red) chowders. Some chowders are very basic, while others have "secret" ingredients or procedures.

- **New England Clam Chowder** (4 to 6 servings)

        3 lb. (1.5 kg) small hardshell clams
        2 cups (500 mL) milk (or light cream)
        $^1/_2$ cup (125 mL) light cream
        $^1/_3$ cup (80 mL) onion, chopped
        3 medium potatoes, peeled and cubed
        2 cups (500 mL) reserved clam broth from cooking the clams
        salt and pepper to taste

(options: add some flour to thicken if desired; spice with thyme and garlic to taste)

Place clams and chopped onion in a large pot, and just cover with cold water. Bring to a boil, and gently simmer until the clams open, about 10 minutes. Strain and reserve the broth. Discard any clams that did not open. Remove clams from the shells and chop them.

In a deep pot, cook potatoes in the reserved broth, season with salt and pepper. Cook until tender, about 15 minutes. Add milk, light cream, and clams, and heat through but do not bring to a boil.

(options: experiment with ingredients—bacon, finely chopped; add butter if you like with milk and cream at the end; use other spices such as oregano; garnish with fresh parsley.)

- **Manhatten Clam Chowder** (4 to 6 servings)

        3 lb. (1.5 kg) small, hardshell clams
        2 cups (500 mL) water or white wine (or combination)
        2 oz. (50 g) salt pork or 3 slices bacon, chopped
        1 medium onion, diced (approx. $^1/_2$ cup or 125 mL)
        3 med. potatoes, peeled and cubed (approx. 2 cups or 500 mL)
        4 med. tomatoes, peeled, seeded, and chopped
        (or one can: 16 oz. or 450 g)
        1 bay leaf
        salt, pepper, thyme to taste

(options: add 1 cup (250 mL) celery, chopped; $^1/_2$ cup green bell pepper, chopped)

Place clams in a large pot with water or wine. Cover and steam over high heat until the shells open, 5 to 10 minutes. Discard any clams that do not open. Reserve the clam broth. Remove the clams from the shells and chop.

In a deep pot, cook salt pork (or bacon) until there is enough fat to sauté the onion (and optional celery). Add the reserved broth, potatoes, tomatoes, bay leaf, salt, pepper, thyme, and enough water to cover. Cover the pot and simmer until the potatoes are tender, about 20 minutes. Add the clams and bring to a boil, then remove from heat. Serve garnished with parsley.

Steamer clams are always a winning offering.

Razor clams

Northern razor clam *Siliqua patula:*
Alaska to central California. Shells to 7 in. (18 cm) long, thin, rounded at the ends. Exterior has an outer covering on the shell, which is a shiny, yellow-tan color. The interior is glossy white with a prominent rib. Found on open, flat sandy beaches that are exposed to surf. Occur at lowest tides, to subtidal depths greater than 33 ft. (10 m).

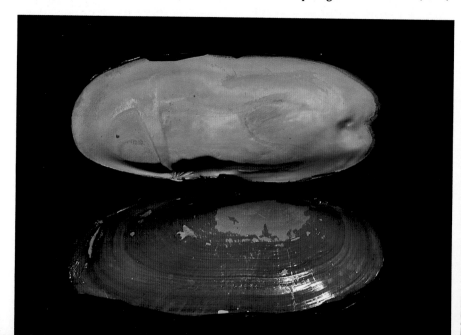

Collection of razor clams

The razor clam is taken by sport and commercial fishermen from Alaska to California. Check with local authorities for the required licenses, open seasons, size limits, and bag limits.

Razor clams leave holes or "shows" when they withdraw their necks and bury themselves. They can be made to show by foot-stomping a dry area or shovel-pounding a wet area. Clams are taken in the surf, "surf digging," in the spring and fall by baring and grasping the neck with one scoop of the shovel. "Dry digging," in the summer, is popular with the use of a "clam gun," (a special shovel), or the use of a corer.

To use the clam-gun shovel, place the blade 4 to 6 in. (10 to 15 cm) seaward of the clam show. Razor clams dig rapidly downward but never horizontally. Push straight down, keeping the blade vertical; remove sand with a lifting motion and twist the shovel at the same time, keeping the blade as vertical as possible. A couple of shovelfuls should expose the clam enough to grasp it.

In many areas, you are required to keep all clams harvested as part of your bag limit. This greatly reduces unnecessary mortalities and losses.

Preparation of razor clams

Remove the shell by submerging the clams in boiling water for a few seconds, or by pouring boiling water over them. When the shells open, plunge the clams immediately into cold water and remove the meats. Remove the dark parts of the clam: the gills and the digestive tract. Snip off the tip of the neck, or siphon, and cut open the clam with a sharp knife or scissors.

Do not be alarmed if you find small crabs ("pea crabs") or flatworms attached to the inside of the clam. They feed on food ingested by the clam but do not affect the clam itself. Simply pick them off and discard.

NOTE: A bulletin on digging techniques, preparation, and cooking razor clams, "Washington State Razor Clams," is available from the Washington State Department of Fisheries, 115 General Administration Building, Olympia, WA 98504. For a northern booklet, contact the Alaska Department of Fish and Game, 333 Raspberry Road, Anchorage, AL 99518.

Cooking of razor clams

Fried razor clam steaks

        razor clam meats
        2 to 3 Tbsp. (30 to 45 mL) butter
        salt and pepper to taste
        $1/4$ cup (60 mL) flour
        1 egg, slightly beaten
        $1/4$ cup (60 mL) cracker crumbs

Melt butter in a skillet. Clams may be fried plain, dipped in flour, or dipped in flour and then the egg and cracker crumbs. Fry quickly, 30 seconds to 1 minute, on each side over high heat. Salt and pepper second side lightly.

Geoduck and horse clams

Geoduck or king clam *Panope abrupta:*
Alaska to Baja. Largest intertidal clam, with fresh weights to 10 lb. (4.5 kg). Shell length is up to 5 in. (13 cm). Siphons are fused, to 4 $^1/4$ ft. (1.3 m) long, and the body cannot be retracted into the shell. The siphon has pale to dark brown (black) skin. Found buried to 4 $^1/4$ ft. (1.3 m) in sand-mud, gravel, and broken shell. Occurs at the lowest tides to depths of 364 ft. (111 m).

Horse clam (gaper, blueneck) *Tresus nuttallii:*
Vancouver Is. to Baja. Large size, with shell length to 8 in. (20 cm). This species has longer shells than *T. capax;* shells are more than 1.5 times as long as they are high. Fresh weights are up to 3 $^1/3$ lb. (1.5 kg). Shells gape. Siphons extend to 20 in. (50 cm) and cannot be retracted into the shell. The siphon tip has two fingernail-like plates, heavier and hardier than those of *T. capax*, and an inner ring of tentacles. Found buried to 20 in. (50 cm) in firm to loose sand-mud. Occurs at low-intertidal zone and subtidally to a 98-ft. (30-m) depth.

Horse clam (gaper, fat gaper, horseneck) *Tresus capax*
Alaska to California. Large size, with shell length to 8 in. (20 cm). Fresh weights to 3 1/3 lb. (1.5 kg). Shells gape; shells are only 1.5 times as long as they are high. Large siphons are fused, and covered with a dark wrinkled skin. The siphon tip has an inner ring of tentacles. Found buried to 20 in. (50 cm) in mud, gravel, and fine sandy mud of bays. Occurs at mid- to lower-intertidal zone, usually higher on the beach than *T. nuttallii.*

The harmless pea crab (shown here on a horse clam) is simply discarded.

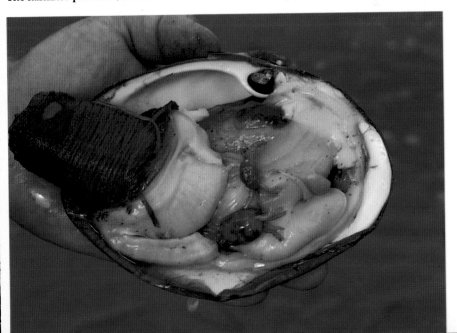

Collection of geoducks or king clams

"Geoduc" is an Indian term meaning "dig deep." And deep these clams are! The body of the geoduck is buried as deep as 3 ft. (one m) in sand, mud, gravel, and broken shell bottoms, with the neck extending to the surface of the substrate.

This clam requires a team approach. Disturbing the clam causes it to retract its long neck, and as it expels water it appears to be digging deeper. When a "show," or neck is spotted, start digging a ring around the clam to about 2 ft. (0.6 m). One clammer has to grasp the neck before it is out of sight and keep a firm grip, but being careful not to pull and break the neck. Be prepared to have your arm pulled down into the burrow (who is catching whom?). The second clammer must dig rapidly to save his companion! It's quite a sport.

Geoducks are harvested commercially with relative ease by divers using hand-held, high-pressure water jets. A water nozzle is guided and controlled by a diver to loosen and wash away the sand surrounding the geoducks. When a geoduck is sighted, the diver exposes the tip of the neck with the water jet, then grasps the neck while he continues to wash away the substrate around the clam until it is freed. A proficient diver can harvest 4 to 6 clams a minute! Sport fishermen are not allowed to use hydraulic or mechanical diggers.

Preparation of geoducks

Cut the clam open by sliding a sharp, thin knife between the body and the shell on both sides; this severs the muscles that close and hold the shells shut. Cut away the viscera and remove the neck and body meat.

King clam necks

Cut off the neck and blanch it in hot water for a minute or more, until the skin peels off freely. Grind the neck or use a food chopper (add slices of raw bacon while grinding if you wish) and use for chowders, casseroles, or clam pie (recipe follows). The primary market for geoducks is Japan, where the necks are sliced thinly and served raw in "sushi" dishes.

Cooking of geoducks

King clam cutlets

The body meat can be cut into thin slices with a sharp knife and fried as described further on for horse clams.

(This recipe for a sour cream clam pie was passed on by the wife of a commercial geoduck fisherman.)

Sour cream clam pie

> 1 lb. (pint or 500 g) geoducks
> ^{1}/3 cup (80 mL) chopped bacon—3 to 4 slices
> ^{3}/4 cup (180 mL) chopped onion
> ^{1}/4 cup (60 mL) flour
> ^{3}/4 cup (180 mL) clam broth (or chicken stock)
> few grains of pepper
> 3 to 4 drops of tabasco

2 eggs, beaten
pastry shell
$^{1}/2$ pint (250 mL) sour cream (or sour cream and yogurt)
1 tsp. (5 mL) salt
paprika to taste

Sauté the onion with the chopped bacon, and oil if necessary. Fry the clams until lightly browned. Blend in flour and add clam broth (or chicken stock). Cook until thick, stirring constantly. Add pepper and tabasco sauce.

Stir a little of the hot sauce into the beaten eggs; then add the mixture back to the remaining sauce, stirring constantly.

Prepare the pie crust; roll; and line a 9-inch pie plate. Place the filling in the pie shell. Combine the sour cream and salt, and spread over the clams. Sprinkle with paprika. Bake at 350°F (200°C) for 30 to 35 minutes or until the filling is set.

Collection of horse clams

Horse clams are readily found at mid to low tides by the "squirt holes" and regular jets of water that shoot to 3 ft. (one m) in the air. The body of the clam may be buried from 10 to 24 in. (25 to 50 cm) deep in the beach. The tip of the siphon may be visible at or above the surface, or you may spot a circular hole up to $1\,^{3}/4$ in. (4.5 cm) in diameter. By poking a finger into the hole, you can feel the neck retract.

Dig the clam out with a shovel, being careful to dig around the clam to avoid cutting the neck or breaking the shell. Horse clams are harvested commercially by divers in the same manner as are geoducks.

Preparation of horse clams

Most horse clams host small "pea crabs." These are harmless to the clam and do not affect their quality. Remove them and discard.

Separate the neck (siphon) from the digger foot. Cut $^{1}/2$ in. (1.25 cm) off the top of the neck and discard. To remove the skin, blanch the neck by dipping it in hot water for approximately a minute, until the skin peels freely. Split the neck lengthwise and wash away the sand and grit.

The tough, rubbery neck can be tenderized and fried but is probably best minced and used in chowders, casseroles, or clam pies: see the recipes for geoducks and clam chowders. The foot is tender and tastes good fried. Cut the digger foot lengthwise, and remove the dark material.

Cooking of horse clams

Fried horse clam

flour
1 egg, well beaten
cracker crumbs

Cover clam parts in flour, dip in beaten egg, and roll in crumbs. Fry in a hot skillet until golden brown, usually no more than 30 seconds per side.

Pacific or Japanese oyster *Crassostrea gigas:*
British Columbia to southern California. Introduced from Japan. Shells, to 12 in. (30 cm), vary: from long and thin when crowded to round and deep when single. The lower, cupped shell is usually cemented to a hard surface; the upper shell is flat. The exterior is rough, usually fluted, chalky, and often with purple streaks. The interior is shiny white. Found in low-intertidal zone of quiet bays, mud flats, and estuaries. Cultured in Japan, British Columbia, Washington, and California.

Oysters

It's always a good idea to shuck your oysters on the beach because the young oysters survive at higher rates when they have oysters shells to settle on.

Native or Olympia oyster *Ostrea lurida:*
Alaska to Baja. Small size, with shells up to $2\,^1/3$ in. (6 cm) long. The thin, circular shell, sometimes with serrated edges, is flat, with both sides equal. The exterior is gray to blue-black, the interior white or greenish-yellow. Found cemented by one shell to rocks or other oyster shells at the low-intertidal zone in quiet bays and estuaries. Cultivated at times in Puget Sound, Washington.

Collection of oysters

The largest and most common oyster, the Pacific oyster, was introduced from Japan in the early 1900s. It now ranges from British Columbia to southern California. Although most oysters are on commercial leases, many populations of wild oysters have resulted from natural local or widespread breedings in years of warm waters and ideal conditions. The smaller native, or "Olympia," oyster is sometimes cultured, but wild stocks are not common.

Oysters can be picked by hand in the low-intertidal zone in sheltered areas with firm mud, sand, or gravel beaches. Gloves are recommended. Shuck the oysters at the beach and discard the shells where you picked them. The juvenile oysters, "spat," can settle and survive at higher rates on oyster shells.

Preparation of oysters

Many harvesters shuck their oysters at the beach (see above), keeping the meat in a sealed container in a cooler. If you take the whole oyster, scrub the shells with a stiff brush under cold running water, but do not leave the oysters in the water.

The easiest way to open the oysters is on the barbecue (see the following recipes). Wear a heavy glove when shucking (opening) oysters. Hold the oyster with the deep or cupped shell down, with the pointed hinge end in your palm. Insert a strong, blunt knife (special oyster knives are available) between the shells an inch or so (2.5 cm) from the hinge end. With a twisting motion, pry the shells open. Try to retain the liquid or "liquor."

An alternate method, used by many to shuck larger oysters, is to hold the oyster in the same position but to insert the knife in the right side about an inch or so (2.5 cm) from the rounded end, and to sever the muscle that holds the shells together. A hammer can be used at the frilly edge to open the shell for the knife to be easily inserted.

When opened, use the knife to cut the muscle holding the two shells together and the muscle holding the oyster to the shell.

Serve the oysters raw on the half shell or drain them, straining the liquor through cheesecloth to remove the particles of shell or sand. Store the oysters and liquor in a tightly sealed container in the refrigerator until ready to use.

Cooking of oysters

Pan-fried oysters (3 to 4 servings)

Any coating on oysters should be minimal so as not to detract from their very distinct flavor. I do not recommend thick batters or deep-frying! Wash oysters well under cold running water and drain well.

> 1 doz. oysters
> $^1/4$ cup (60 mL) flour
> 1 egg, slightly beaten with 1 Tbsp. (15 mL) milk
> $^1/4$ cup (60 mL) plain cracker crumbs
> 2 to 3 Tbsp. (30 to 45 mL) butter
> salt and pepper to taste

Melt butter in a skillet. Dip oysters in flour, then in beaten egg, and roll in cracker crumbs. Fry over medium heat, until the edges of the oysters curl. Add the salt and pepper.

Oyster soup "New Orleans" (4 servings)

> 1 doz. oysters
> 1 stalk celery, chopped finely
> 1 cup (250 mL) water (or $^1/2$ water and $^1/2$ white wine)
> 2 cups (500 mL) scalded milk
> 1 Tbsp. (15 mL) melted butter, blended with 1 Tbsp. (15 mL) flour
> salt and pepper to taste

Simmer the chopped celery in water (or water-wine mix) for 25 minutes. Add oysters with their liquor and cook gently for 5 minutes or until their edges begin to curl. Remove the oysters, cut them into bite-size pieces. Return the oysters to the pot, adding the scalded milk. Thicken with butter-flour mixture. Season and serve garnished with parsley.

Barbecued oysters

Better than shucking, just place oysters, rounded shell down, on the grill 3 to 4 in. (7 to 10 cm) above the hot coals. When the shells open, usually in 10 to 15 minutes, pry them off gently, sprinkle with lemon juice, and serve.

Pink and spiny scallops are as colorful as they are tasty.

Oysters on the barbecue is a good reason for a get-together at any time on the Pacific Coast.

California (giant, sea) mussel *Mytilus californianus:*

Alaska to southern Baja. Large size, with shells to 5 in. (13 cm) long intertidally, and to 10 in. (25 cm) offshore, subtidally. The thick shells are pointed at one end, and rounded at the other, featuring strong radial ribs; the surface is often worn or eroded. There is a heavy covering of blue-black on the outer shell, and the interior is blue-gray, slightly iridescent. The mussel has bright orange flesh. Found firmly attached to rocks by fibers from the foot ("beard"). Occurs intertidally on surf-exposed rocks; also subtidally and offshore on reefs to 79 ft. (24 m) deep.

Mussels

Collection of mussels
Mussels can be gathered from the rocks, by hand or by using hand tools, during most low tides. Avoid mussels that may have been out of the water for long periods of time and exposed to sunlight and air. Mussels should be eaten as soon as possible after harvest. Refrigerate but do not keep for several days before you prepare them.

The bay or blue mussel is found in most protected waters, while the California mussel is found only on exposed, open coast shores. Blue mussels are cultured throughout Europe and recently on both coasts of North America. They are marketed fresh, frozen, canned, or smoked and canned.
(See the section on PSP)

Bay (blue) mussel *Mytilus edulis:*

Arctic Ocean to Baja.; west coast of S. America; Japan; Australia; N. Atlantic. Small to medium size, with shell length to 4 in. (10 cm). Its long, thin shells are nearly smooth. Blue-black, sometimes brown. The interior is dull blue. Found in the mid-intertidal zone, in more protected waters than the California mussel. Common on rocks and fouling buoys, floats, pilings, and wharves. Cultivated for food in Europe and North America.

Preparation of mussels

Discard any mussels with gaping shells that do not close when the inside is prodded. Scrape or rub off any encrusting growths, remove the beard (the attaching fibers) with a quick pull, and wash under cold running water. Like many clams, mussels sometimes host small "pea crabs," which are harmless and do not affect their host's quality. Discard them.

If taken from a sandy area, soak mussels in salted water (1 1/2 Tbsp. or 25 mL of salt to 1 liter or 4 cups tap water) for 30 minutes to an hour, changing the water every 15 to 20 minutes. The shells may be opened with a knife but are usually steamed open. The characteristic color of mussel meat is bright orange when cooked. The entire meat is edible (except for the thread-like beard).

Cooking of mussels

Mussels on the barbecue

Scrub and clean as above. Place mussels on the grill 3 to 4 in. (7 to 10 cm) above hot coals and heat until the shells open, in 5 to 10 minutes. Sprinkle lemon and melted butter on the mussel meats and serve in the half-shell.

Steamed mussels

Allow 6 to 12 mussels per person.

Place the mussels in a steamer or sieve over rapidly boiling water. Steam until the shells are open and the meat is coming loose from the shell: 5 to 10 minutes. Serve with lemon juice or lemon butter.

Mussels in mussel broth

Allow 6 to 12 mussels per person.
2 garlic cloves, pressed
3 shallots, chopped (or the white part of green onions)
3 Tbsp. (45 mL) olive oil
1 cup (250 mL) dry white wine (or water)
several sprigs fresh parsley, minced
ground pepper to taste

In a large pot, sauté garlic cloves, shallots (or the white part of green onions) in olive oil. Add dry white wine (or water), minced parsley (optional), and fresh ground pepper to taste. Add the mussels and bring to a boil, then simmer for 8 to 10 minutes until the shells open. Discard any mussels that do not open. Spoon mussels into individual bowls and pour remaining broth over them.

(options: The meat can be dipped into melted butter with lemon juice, or butter seasoned with garlic and parsley.)

Mussel broth, mussel bisque

3 lb. (1.25 kg) mussels in the shell
2 cups (500 mL) water (or part wine)
1 Tbsp. (15 mL) onion, chopped
1 Tbsp. (15 mL) celery, chopped
1 Tbsp. (15 mL) parsley, minced
salt, pepper and melted butter to taste.

Steam the mussels in water with the onion and celery until the shells open: 5 to 10 minutes. Season and serve mussels in the shell. Save the vegetables for rice dishes to accompany any meal. Save the strained liquid to be served as mussel broth, or to be thickened into mussel bisque.

For mussel bisque:

mussel broth (from above)
milk or light cream
1 Tbsp. (15 mL) parsley

Add an equal amount of milk or light cream to mussel broth. Thicken with a paste of flour and melted butter if desired. Heat (do not bring to boil), and serve, sprinkled with parsley.

Scallops

Collection of scallops

Very occasionally rock scallops occur intertidally and can be gathered at the lowest tides. Other scallops are strictly subtidal and are taken recreationally by diving. Commercially, scallops are harvested in deep water by the use of bottom drags and, in the case of the pink scallops, by diving. Unlike clams and many other bivalves, the adductor muscles that open and close the scallop shell are fused together. The small, tough, opaque muscle on the outer side of the large muscle is removed and discarded. The meat is marketed in fresh, frozen, and breaded forms.

Preparation of scallops

Rock scallops: With your diver's knife, or a small hammer, break off a piece of the shell at the margin. It is then easy to insert a sturdy knife between the shells and to cut the muscle holding the shells together. Carefully run the knife close to the shell, top and bottom, and the meat will slide out of the shell. Cut out and clean the large, circular muscle. Wash it quickly under cold running water, removing any bits of shell or sand. Remove the small, tough, opaque muscle on the outer side of the scallop meat and discard it. Cut large scallops in half, or into slices.

Scallop fresh out of the water is delicious eaten raw with lemon juice. The "roe" (generally refers to both male and female gonads) is edible, and can be marinated (with 2 Tbsp. or 30 mL lemon juice and $^1/2$ cup or 125 mL olive oil, turning frequently), and served on crackers.

Pink and spiny scallops: Scrub the sponge off with a bristle brush. These can then be steamed open like clams or opened and cooked on the barbecue. All of the scallop can be eaten, like a steamer clam, or just the muscle meat or "button."

Pink and spiny scallops are found subtidally and are taken by divers.

Rock scallop *Crassadoma giganteus:*
Queen Charlotte Islands to Baja. Large rounded shell, with heights to 6 in. (15 cm)
intertidally, and up to 10 in. (25 cm) subtidally. Juveniles are free swimming, while
adults cement themselves to substrate. Shells are thick and heavy, the upper shell
having strong ribs, each with fluted spines. Winglike extensions appear at the hinge.
The rock scallop is often eroded by a yellow boring sponge and encrusted with heavy
growths. The interior of its shell is pearly white with a purple blotch at the hinge. The
rock scallop features a large, edible adductor muscle. Found intertidally to subtidal
depths of 164 ft. (50 m), on rocks, in crevices, on pilings. Sports fishery only. Common
but not abundant.

Pink (smooth) scallop *Chlamys rubida:*
Alaska to central California. Small shell to 2 1/3 in. (6 cm) high, with smooth radial ribs,
and winglike extensions at the hinge. One shell is a pink-rose color, the other almost
white. The adductor muscle is small, and the whole animal is usually eaten. Found
subtidally on rocky and gravel bottoms. Free-swimming.

Pink (spiny) scallop *Chlamys hastata:*
Northern B.C. to Baja. Small shell, with a height of up to 2 $^1/_2$ in. (6.5 cm). Spiny radial ribs are a feature, with the secondary radial ribs raised about half as high. The shells are often overgrown by an orange or purple sponge. Winglike extensions appear at the hinge. Pink-rose shells identify this scallop, with one shell being darker than the other; the inside is white with rose on the margin. The adductor muscle is small, and the whole animal is usually eaten. Found subtidally on rocky and gravel bottoms. Free-swimming. Often taken by divers.

Weathervane scallop *Patinopectin caurinus:*
Alaska to Oregon. Large shell, with a height of up to 9 in. (23 cm). One shell is convex, with a yellow-tan color; the other shell is almost flat. Winglike extensions appear at the hinge of this free-swimming scallop. The inside is a glossy, or sometimes dull, white. The adductor muscle is large. Found subtidally to 360 ft. (110 m) on sand and mud bottoms. Taken in bottom drags by fishing vessels, occasionally by divers.

Cooking of scallops

Pan-fried scallops (3 or 4 servings)

> 1 lb. (500 g) scallops
> 2 Tbsp. (30 mL) butter
> 2 Tbsp. (30 mL) chopped onions
> $1/4$ tsp. (1 mL) each paprika, thyme, oregano
> parsley and lemon wedges.
> salt and pepper to taste

In a skillet melt butter, add spices, and sauté onion. Add scallops and sauté over high heat, turning occasionally for 5 to 7 minutes. Serve with parsley and lemon wedges.

Baked scallops (or curried scallops)

> 1 lb. (500 g) scallops
> $1/4$ cup (60 mL) cracker crumbs or fine, dry bread crumbs
> 3 Tbsp. (45 mL) butter
> 2 tsp. (10 mL) lemon juice
> thin lemon slices to garnish

(options: 1 tsp. (5 mL) curry powder to mix with melted butter)

Preheat oven to 450°F (230°C).
Butter 4 large scallop shells or shallow individual baking dishes. Rinse scallops under cold running water and dry well. Roll each scallop in bread crumbs, coating with crumbs on all sides. Arrange scallops in a single layer in the baking dishes or shells.

Melt butter in a small saucepan, add curry (optional) and cook gently, stirring, for about 2 minutes. Stir in lemon juice. Drizzle over scallops. Lay a sliver of lemon on top of each serving. Bake about 10 to 15 minutes or until scallops are tender.

Coquilles St. Jacques (4 servings)

Although this is a recipe that demands more time, effort, and ingredients than most covered in this book, the resulting dish is well worth it!

> 1 lb. (500 g) scallops
> $1/2$ cup (125 mL) water and $1/2$ cup dry white wine or vermouth
> $1/2$ tsp. (2 mL) crushed dried thyme
> 1 bay leaf
> 1 parsley sprig
> 4 shallots or 4 green onions (white part only), chopped
> $1/4$ cup (60 mL) fresh mushrooms, sliced
> 1 Tbsp. (15 mL) butter
> 1 tsp. (5 mL) fresh lemon juice
> 2 Tbsp. (30 mL) butter
> 2 Tbsp. (30 mL) flour
> $1/2$ cup (125 mL) light cream
> 1 egg yolk
> $1/4$ cup (60 mL) soft bread crumbs
> 2 Tbsp. (30 mL) grated cheddar cheese

Wash scallops, drain, and dry well. Bring water and wine with herbs and $^1/2$ of the onions to a boil. Add scallops, salt and pepper to taste, and simmer for 6 to 8 minutes or until the scallops turn opaque. Drain and save the broth for later. Cut up large scallops or cut all into small pieces. Preheat oven to 425°F (220°C). In a large frying pan, sauté the remaining onions and the mushrooms in butter and lemon juice for about one minute. Save.

Melt butter in a saucepan (double boiler if available) and blend in flour. Pour in the reserved scallop broth; cook and stir until thickened.

Mix cream with slightly beaten egg yolk and add to the sauce. Stir in scallops, mushrooms, and onions. Pour into 4 greased scallop shells (or shallow individual baking dishes). Sprinkle with bread crumbs and cheese. Bake in preheated oven at 425°F (220°C) for 8 to 10 minutes, or just until lightly browned.

Baked scallops served on the shell and topped with lemon butter is a favorite recipe for a quick and tasty meal.

Abalone

Check local fisheries regulations for seasons, area closures, size limits, bag limits and other restrictions.

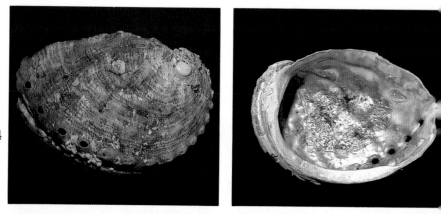

Northern (pinto) abalone *Haliotis kamtschatkana:*
Alaska to central California. Medium in size, with shell length to 6 in. (15 cm). The thin shells have a rough, wavy exterior and are red or greenish-brown. The interior is iridescent green, blue, and lavender. Shell holes are oval; 4 to 6 holes usually remain open. Found in rocky, kelp habitats, intertidally and subtidally to 2 $^1/_4$ ft. (7 m) on protected and exposed shores.

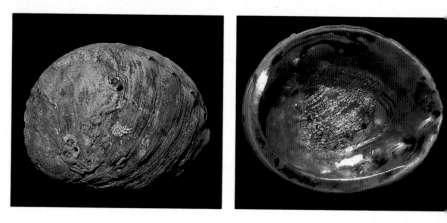

Red abalone *Haliotis rufescens:*
Oregon to Baja, especially central California. Large shell length is up to 12 in. (30 cm), with the exterior being irregular; usually brick red, and often overgrown with organisms. Shell holes are oval, raised, and usually 3 or 4 remain open. Found in rocky, heavy surf areas, intertidally to depths of over 590 ft. (180 m)! Commercial fishery at 20 to 56 ft. (6 to 17 m) depths. Preliminary mariculture in California.

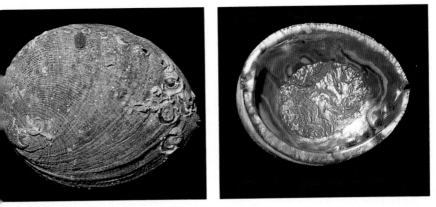

Green abalone *Haliotis fulgens:*
Conception Pt., CA, to Baja. Large, with shell length to 10 in. (25 cm), featuring fine spiral ribs; the exterior is olive-green to reddish-brown, the interior strongly iridescent green, blue, and lavender. Shell holes are circular, 5 to 7 remaining open. Common in rocky areas, and in crevices, exposed to strong wave action.

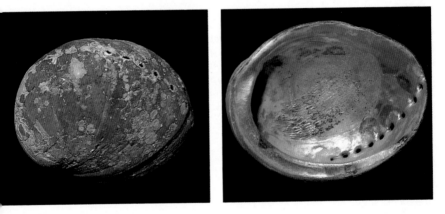

Black abalone *Haliotis cracherodii:*
Oregon to Baja. Large, with shell length to 8 in. (20 cm), smooth, usually free of growth. The exterior is dark blue, green, or nearly black. Shell holes are not raised, 5 to 7 remaining open. The interior is pearly-pink and iridescent green. Common, occurring higher in the intertidal zone than other abalone, to depths of 20 ft. (6 m). Found under rocks and in crevices.

Collection of abalone

Abalone numbers have declined in many areas, so please check for local regulations and size limits.

Some species can be taken on very low tides, but usually only in more remote areas where there is little fishing. Most abalone are landed by skin or scuba divers using a special "ab" tool, or blunt diving knife. A mark should be made on the knife or tool indicating the legal size, and care should be taken not to damage or cut sublegal size abalone. Size measurements should be made underwater before attempting to harvest.

It is very easy to cut the foot of the abalone, causing "bleeding" and often mortality. When undersize abalone are thrown overboard, they may be easy prey until regaining a safe position. If taken, sublegals must be returned immediately to their original rock position.

An abalone that is not firmly clamped to a rock is removed by quickly slipping the knife under it to break the suction of its foot on the bottom and flipping it up in the water. Abalone are marketed live, frozen, or processed into steaks and frozen, canned in brine, or canned in soups. Abalone shells are used in various handicrafts.

Preparation of abalone

When possible, abalone will be far more tender if left in the shell in the refrigerator overnight in a container, covered with a wet cloth. Freezing also results in tenderizing.

Shuck the abalone out of the shell by pushing a strong tablespoon or blunt knife (ab "poppers" are commercially available) under the meat, keeping it in contact with the shell. This should clean the shell of white meat. Trim off the green intestines, the dark areas, and fringes, and cut out the mouth and anus at opposite ends on the underside. Slice the body meat $1/4$ in. thick and tenderize by pounding with a meat hammer.

Cooking of abalone

Pan-fried abalone steaks

abalone steaks, sliced to $1/4$ in. (0.6 cm) thick
2 to 3 Tbsp. (30 to 45 mL) butter
salt and pepper to taste
$1/4$ cup (60 mL) flour
1 egg, slightly beaten
$1/4$ cup (60 mL) cracker crumbs

In a skillet, melt butter. Abalone may be fried plain, dipped in flour, or dipped in flour and then in the egg and cracker crumbs. Fry quickly, 30 seconds to 1 minute on each side over high heat. Salt and pepper second side lightly. Cooking longer will make the abalone tough.

Squid

Collection of squid

Squid are usually fished at night under lights by squid jigs, dip nets, or by beach seining. They are harvested commercially by a variety of techniques, including seine or lampara nets, midwater and bottom trawls, gillnets, and jigs. They have been landed in California since the late 1800s, initially by the Chinese using small purse seines. In recent years limited fisheries have taken place in Oregon, Washington, and British Columbia.

Preparation of squid

The mantle, tail, arms, and tentacles of the squid are all edible and comprise 60 to 80% of the total weight. This recovery weight is better than most finfish (20 to 50%). The ink from squid is sometimes refined and used by artists. Squid spoil very rapidly, so care must be taken in handling and processing the catch. The skin tears easily and the ink sac ruptures. The quicker squid are cleaned (and frozen), the better their quality.

Wash the squid well under cold, running water. Hold the tentacles in one hand and the pointed body section in the other. Separate the head and tentacle section from the body by pulling gently.

• Head section: Cut off and save the tentacles and arms, just below the eye, discarding the eye section. Squeeze out the "beak," a small round cartilage at the base of the tentacles, and discard.

• Body section: The ink sac can be removed intact and saved for sauces. Rinse and discard the contents of the mantle or body; pull out and discard the long transparent "quill" from inside the body. Pull off and discard the transparent, speckled membrane that covers the body.

Wash and dry the edible portions of the tentacles and body. The body can be left whole and stuffed with various fillings, or cut into rings (cutting across the body at 1-inch intervals), or cut along the entire length of the body and flattened into a "steak" to be breaded.

Cooking of squid

Barbecued squid

> 3 lb. (1.5 kg) squid, cleaned, cut into rings
> melted butter with lemon/garlic

Skewer the squid rings. Barbecue for 2 to 3 minutes each side, 3 to 4 in. (7 to 10 cm) over hot coals. Serve hot with melted butter, lemon.

Sautéed squid (4 servings)

> 3 lb. (1.5 kg) whole squid, cleaned and cut into flat pieces (yields 2 lb. or 1 kg meat)
> 1 cup (250 mL) flour
> 2 cups (500 mL) cracker or breadcrumbs
> 1 egg
> ^{1}/2 cup (125 mL) milk
> 6 Tbsp. (90 mL) butter
> salt and pepper to taste
> parsley, chopped
> lemon wedges
> *(Continued)*

Opalescent (opal or market) squid *Loilgo opalescens:*
British Columbia to Mexico. Total length (including the arms and tentacles) is 10 to 14 in. (25 to 35 cm); the males are generally larger. There are 2 long tentacles and 8 arms. The body is cylindrical, with 2 fins about half as long as the mantle, and is translucent bluish-white changing to mottled browns and reds. Found in open coastal waters, but aggregate and spawn in shallow inshore areas. Common; sometimes spawns and deposits eggs intertidally. Attracted by lights at night. The life span is 1 to 3 years.

Rinse under cold running water, drain, and dry well. Cover lightly with flour. Dip into lightly beaten egg and milk mixture to coat thoroughly, put into bag of cracker or breadcrumbs, and shake vigorously.

Melt butter in a large, heavy frying pan. Fry squid, in a single layer, over high heat until browned, then turn over. Serve immediately, garnished with chopped parsley and lemon wedges, salt and pepper.

Squid jigs.

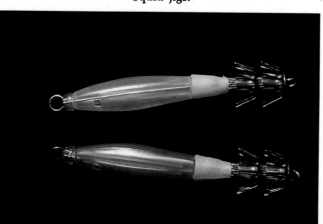

Dungeness crab *Cancer magister:*
Alaska to California. Carapace (shell) grows to a width of 13 in. (33 cm) in males, and to 6 $\frac{1}{2}$ in. (16.6 cm) in females. Weights go to 4 $\frac{1}{2}$ lb. (2 kg). Ten teeth appear along each leading edge of the shell, which is grayish-brown, sometimes with a purple tinge; the legs and underside are brownish-white (turns red when cooked). Abundant on firm sand-mud bottoms; taken in traps at 30 to 150 ft. (10 to 45 m). Supports a large fishery from British Columbia to California.

Crustaceans

Red rock crab *Cancer productus:*
Alaska to San Diego, CA. This is a smaller crab, with a carapace, or shell, width to 6 $\frac{1}{4}$ in. (16 cm) in both sexes. The front margin has broad, rounded teeth. It is dark reddish-purple on top, with a yellowish-white underside, and black tips on the claws. Common in shallow waters in eelgrass beds, sand, mud and gravel bays, and rocky shores. Found to subtidal depths of 245 ft. (79 m). Popular sport fishery but not found in commercial abundance.

Crabs

Collection of crabs

Red rock crab is not as abundant as the Dungeness crab, though many are taken in shallow waters, just below the low tide line, in ring nets or folding crab traps. Red rock crabs are found in eelgrass beds and most shallow bays. There is a minimum size limit in B.C. of 4 1/2 in. (11.5 cm) across the carapace from point to point, and 4 in. (10 cm) across the shell in California. (Washington and Oregon did not have a size limit at the time of writing).

Dungeness crabs show a definite preference for firm sand bottoms but are found over muddy sand as well. They are found around the mouths of bays, inlets, tidal flats, and tidal streams. Try fishing at the seaward edge of low tide and move deeper. Trapping is usually more successful at high or low slack tides. The crabs are trapped commercially at depths of 30 to 150 ft. (10 to 45 m). Traps are left in the water for 1 to 10 days.

Both crab species are taken by ring or hoop traps, folding traps, skin or scuba diving, or dipnetting at low tides. It is prohibited to use sharp, pointed instruments, rakes or spears that would damage crabs that are undersize or that might cause their injury and allow their escape. The best baits are fish heads and carcasses, herring or clams. The Dungeness crab feeds mainly on small clams, opened by chipping at the shell with the claws.

It is prohibited in many regions to take females, and the minimum size limit effectively protects the slower-growing and smaller females from being taken in the fishery. Restrictions vary from area to area, so always check the local sport-fishing regulations. Some minimum size limits for Dungeness crabs are: in B.C., 6 1/2 in. (16.5 cm) across the greatest breadth of the shell, including the points; in the States, the measurement is taken immediately in front of and not including the points: 6 in. (15.24 cm) in Washington, 5 3/4 in. (14.5 cm) in Oregon, and 6 1/4 in. (16 cm) in California.

Preparation of crabs

Crabs can be cleaned before cooking, or they can be dropped alive into a large pot of boiling water and cleaned after cooking. The following cleaning method can be used for either live or cooked crabs:

Lay the crab on its back and cut up the middle of the flap—a light blow with your hand or a mallet may be required to break through the undershell (do not cut right through the crab to top shell).

Grasp a set of legs in each hand and twist them, one at a time, away from the shell to bring the attached body meat with them. The top shell and the viscera should be left behind.

(Continued)

Cooking of crabs

Steamed cracked crab

> Dungeness crabs: allow 1 lb. (500 g) per person
> or 1 large crab for 2 people
> melted butter with lemon wedges
> sourdough bread or rolls

Fill a deep pot with enough fresh water to completely cover the crabs. Salt with up to 1 Tbsp. (15 mL) salt for each quart (liter) of water. Bring to a boil. Dunk live crabs or cleaned halves into the water, cover, and bring water back to a boil. Reduce heat and simmer about 15 minutes per pound (most crabs weigh $1 \frac{1}{2}$ to $3 \frac{1}{2}$ lb. (0.68 to 1.6 kg) whole). Do not overcook.

Remove and plunge crabs into clean, cold water, then drain well. Serve crab pieces on a large platter, accompanied with individual dishes of melted butter and lemon wedges, and the bread or rolls.

Toasted crab and cheese sandwiches (4 servings)

> 4 sourdough rolls, cut in half and buttered
> $\frac{1}{2}$ lb. (250 g) flaked cooked crab meat
> 4 oz. (125 g) Gruyere or Jarlsberg cheese, shredded
> 1/2 cup (125 mL) sour cream
> 2 green onions, chopped
> freshly ground pepper to taste

Cut, butter, and lightly toast rolls. Mix crab, shredded cheese, and sour cream. Spread on top of each half roll. Sprinkle chopped green onions and ground pepper on top to taste. Heat through and lightly brown in a preheated oven at 400°F (210°C).

Steamed crab is delicious served on lettuce with lemon slices.

Steamed prawns always mouth-watering and utterly delicious.

Shrimp and prawns

Prawn or spot shrimp *Pandalus platyceros:*
Alaska to northern California. With a total length to 12 in. (30 cm), this is the largest shrimp found in the north Pacific. It is characterized by a stout body and two large spots on each of the first and fifth abdominal sections. Taken by divers or in traps at night on rocky bottoms at depths of 100 ft. or 17 fathoms (30 m) and deeper. Only a small percentage are taken in bottom trawls for other shrimps.

Coonstripe or dock shrimp *Pandalus danae:*
Alaska to California. Total body length to 5 $^{1}/_{2}$ in. (14 cm). Recognized by its stout body and irregular brown or red striping and spots, and dark banded legs. Autumn sport fishery from docks at night with traps or baited rings. Also taken in traps on sand and gravel bottoms, usually in areas with moderate to strong currents, at 12 to 600 ft. or 2 to 100 fathoms (4 to 180 m).

(Spiny) pink shrimp *Pandalus borealis:*
Circumpolar, to Oregon on the Pacific coast, and to Massachusetts on the Atlantic; U.S.S.R., and Japan. Slender, compressed body with a prominent spine pointing backwards on the third abdominal segment. Found on muddy bottoms at 60 to 2,100 ft. or 10 to 350 fathoms (18 to 640 m). Sometimes taken in traps; harvested commercially by bottom trawls.

Collection of shrimp and prawns

Prawns: Fishing for prawns is a difficult and often secretive sport. Fishing locations, depths, and fishing or soak times vary seasonally and geographically. You may find it useful to keep a record of your fishing trials.

Most prawns are trapped at depths of 50 to 500 ft. or 9 to 80 fathoms (15 to 150 m) in rocky areas that provide shelter to the prawns. A soak time of 4 to 6 hours at least is recommended. If fishing at dusk or overnight, you can fish shallower at 60 to 120 ft. or 10 to 20 fathoms (18 to 37 m) for 3 to 4 hours, as prawns move up in response to the decreased light.

Homemade traps of unpainted plywood or cedar lathe are heavier but generally as effective as commercially available traps. Common baits are fresh or frozen herring, dogfish or other fish carcasses, and canned sardines. Most traps will yield an average catch of $^1/_2$ to 1 lb. (250 to 500 g), or 10 to 15 prawns. Divers often hunt for prawns on night dives, using forks to spear prawns or other shrimp.

In most areas you are required to have a float with your name on it marking each trap. Inquire at local fisheries offices or with sport-fishing guides for regulations.

Shrimp: Some of the most productive and least expensive fishing is done with homemade metal ring traps or hoops of about 2 ft. (60 cm) in diameter. A burlap sack or fine netting is stretched over the ring to form a shallow basket. A rope is tied to 4 places on the ring to make a sling with which to pull up the trap. Commercially made shrimp pots and traps are available at hardware and sporting-goods stores, though cedar-box or unpainted-plywood traps can also be made at home.

Set the traps in shallow water, to depths of 90 ft. or 15 fathoms (30 m). Popular baits are fish carcasses, clams, or canned sardines. There is an autumn sports fishery for coonstripe or dock shrimp from docks at night, fishing baited hoops or rings at 6 to 12 ft. or 1 to 2 fathoms (2 to 4 m). The shrimp feed after sunset and seem to move in "waves." Set and pull the traps every 10 to 15 minutes.

In some areas, people shrimp along the beach at night, finding the shrimp by shining a light in the water. The shrimps' eyes reflect the light and appear to glow! A fine dip net or a kitchen sieve can be used to scoop up a feed.

Preparation of shrimp and prawns

One pound (500 g) of fresh or frozen shrimp in the shell yields approximately $^1/_2$ lb. (250 g) shelled, cooked meat. Shrimp or prawns may be shelled and deveined before or after cooking. Wash fresh shrimp before cooking. Leave to cool when they are cooked; do not rinse them in cold water, as much of the flavor will be lost. Shell when cooled.

Cooking of shrimp and prawns

Steamed or boiled shrimp or prawns in the shell

• **Steamed:** Place shrimp in a vegetable steamer or sieve over rapidly boiling water, until they turn red: 3 minutes for small shrimp or 5 minutes for large shrimp or prawns.

• **Boiled:** Cover the shrimp in well-salted water (2 tsp. or 10 mL salt if shelled, and 1 Tbsp. or 15 mL if not shelled, for each quart or liter of water). Bring to a boil, then reduce heat and simmer approximately 5 minutes for small shrimp, or 8 minutes for larger shrimp or prawns.

NOTE: Overcooking makes the meat mushy and difficult to extract from the shell. In these recipes, you may substitute the equivalent amount of prawns where shrimp is called for.

Shrimp pilaff (4 servings)

> 1 lb. (500 g) large shrimp in the shell
> 2 cups (500 mL) fish stock, clam nectar, or water
> 1 medium onion, chopped
> 2 stalks celery, chopped
> 3 Tbsp. (45 mL) olive oil
> 1 cup (250 mL) long-grain rice
> 2 medium tomatoes, peeled, seeded, and chopped
> salt and ground pepper to taste
> $^1/4$ cup (60 mL) butter
> minced fresh parsley or dried flakes

Bring fish stock to boil and use to steam shrimp for 5 minutes or until shrimp turn pink. Remove shrimp and let cool (do not rinse), then shell. Reserve the broth.

In an 8-cup or 2-liter casserole dish, sauté onion and celery in olive oil until soft. Add rice and cook on low heat until rice is opaque and coated with oil. Add 2 cups of the reserved broth and tomatoes to the rice dish. Bring to a boil and simmer, covered, for 20 to 25 minutes. In the last few minutes, place the shrimp on top of the rice to heat them.

In a small saucepan, heat butter until sizzling and lightly browned, then pour over shrimp and rice. Garnish with parsley and serve immediately with salt and pepper.

Shrimp bisque (6 servings)

> 1 lb. (500 g) fresh whole shrimp;
> or: $^1/2$ lb. (250 g) shelled, cooked meat
> 2 Tbsp. (30 mL) celery, chopped
> 2 Tbsp. (30 mL) carrot, chopped
> 2 Tbsp. (30 mL) onion, chopped
> 2 fresh mushrooms, chopped
> 3 Tbsp. (45 mL) butter
> 2 cups (500 mL) fish stock (or chicken bouillon)
> $^1/2$ bay leaf
> $^1/2$ tsp. (2 mL) tarragon
> sprinkle of nutmeg
> salt and ground pepper to taste
> 1 cup (250 mL) light cream
> splash of dry wine or sherry
> minced parsley and paprika

Steam shrimp for 5 minutes or until they turn pink, and drain. In a deep pot, sauté celery, carrot, onion, and mushrooms in butter. Add stock and seasonings. Simmer for 15 minutes; strain and discard vegetables (or, better, use in a rice dish). Chop and add shrimp. Simmer for 5 minutes. Add cream and wine, and heat through but do not boil. Serve immediately. Sprinkle servings with minced parsley and paprika.

There is a lot of delectable meat in a steamed goose-neck barnacle.

Barnacles

Giant barnacles *Balanus nubilus:*
   Southern Alaska to central California. This large barnacle runs to 4 ¹/3 in. (11 cm) in diameter, and 5 in. (13 cm) high, with well-developed ribs on the shell, often eroded on older individuals. Cemented calcareous base; the top rim is jagged. A large shell "beak" projects at the top. Found at the low-intertidal zone to 295 ft. (90 m) deep, on rocks and pilings; usually in areas of moderate to strong currents.

Goose (goose-neck) barnacles *Pollicipes polymerus:*
British Columbia to Baja. Small to medium size in stalk length, to 6 in. (15 cm). The edible stalk is crowned by 5 white plates and numerous calcareous scales. Occurring in clusters, goose barnacles feed by sweeping pairs of legs or "cirri." Found in the mid- to low-tidal range on surf-pounded rocks. Often mixed with California mussels (also edible).

• **In collecting** the barnacles, which can be broken off rocks in clusters at low tides (see picture, p. 63), take care to minimize damage to the stalks.

• **To prepare** goose barnacles (below), brush off any encrusting growths, and wash them thoroughly under running water. Cook as soon as possible, though barnacles can be stored temporarily.

Collection of barnacles

Giant barnacles can usually be broken off in clusters at the lowest tides, and can be taken while diving.

Goose barnacles are harvested at low tides from the rocks. Sometimes the easiest method is to remove them when they are growing on or with a cluster of mussels. A strong knife, like a diving knife, or special chisels, can be used to pry them loose. Try to minimize the cuts or damage to the stalks.

Preparation of barnacles

Giant barnacles: Scrape and brush off any encrusting growths. Probably the best method is to cook the whole barnacle on an open fire, as the native Indians did. Remove the operculum (shell "beak"), and eat the meat out of the shell.

Goose barnacles: Cook as soon as possible. They can be stored for a short period, covered with a damp cloth in the refrigerator. Wash the barnacles thoroughly under cold running water, particularly the area where the base was attached.

Cooking of barnacles

Steamed goose barnacles (appetizer)

Bring water to a boil. Place whole barnacles in a sieve or steamer, cover, and steam for 20 minutes. Remove the barnacles from the pot, gently pull the crown, and strip off the leathery skin; discard. Detach the bite-size meat, now reddish-orange in color, from the crown and dip it in butter with garlic or lemon.

Barnacle chowders

Barnacles can be cooked as above and substituted for other shellfish in chowders: see the shrimp bisque or sea cucumber chowder for examples.

❏ ❏ ❏

Five edible muscle strips are attached to the inside of the sea cucumber body wall.

(Continued) →

Echinoderms

Sea cucumber

Collection of sea cucumbers

This, our largest sea cucumber (see picture, page 50), may be found in shallow water on low tides and may be gathered, sometimes, by wading, or in deeper water by skin or scuba diving. It is a slow-moving, sluggish animal generally, but can move quickly in an escape response to seastar predators. Don't be surprised if the animal expels water, and often its internal parts, as this is a unique defense mechanism to decoy would-be predators. Sea cucumbers are commercially harvested by divers.

Preparation of sea cucumbers

With a sharp filleting knife, cut off both ends of the body, and squeeze out the internal organs. Cut the body open lengthwise and remove the 5 long white muscle strips by sliding the knife, or your finger, under and along the length of the muscle (see picture, page 48). Because the body wall of the local sea cucumber is thin compared to the Oriental sea cucumbers, it is usually discarded and only the muscle strips are used. Some fish markets may sell dried sea cucumber from the Orient that includes the body wall; these are called "trepang."

Cooking of sea cucumbers

Fried sea cucumber muscle strips

Wash the muscle strips under cold running water, drain, and dry well. The muscle strips can be fried plain or dipped in flour and quickly cooked over high heat in butter for about 1 minute. Plain muscle strips can be fried and seasoned with lemon juice or soya sauce.

Sea cucumber chowders

Sea cucumbers can be used as a substitute in other soups and chowders.

    muscle strips from 6 sea cucumbers
    2 Tbsp. (30 mL) butter
    1 cup (250 mL) onion, chopped
    1 cup (250 mL) fresh mushrooms, sliced
    1 cup (250 mL) carrots, chopped
    3 cups (750 mL) fish stock (or chicken stock)
    1 cup (250 mL) sour cream
    2 Tbsp. (30 mL) flour
    $1/2$ tsp. (2.5 mL) dill
    salt and pepper to taste
    parsley, chopped

Chop and sauté sea cucumber muscle strips in butter with vegetables for 5 minutes. Add stock and simmer for 15 minutes. Blend in remaining ingredients. Cook over medium heat, stirring constantly until thickened. Garnish servings with parsley.

California sea cucumber *Parastichopus californicus:*
Alaska to Baja. Large, to about 20 in. (50 cm) long. The soft, cylindrical body has numerous soft, fleshy projections, and white oral tentacles. The upper body is mottled orange, red, and brown; the underside is yellow. The cucumber has 5 edible muscle strips attached to the inside of the body wall. Common and abundant on both rocky and soft substrates, from the lower-intertidal zone to subtidal depths of 295 ft. (90 m) or more.

Sea urchins

Red sea urchin *Strongylocentrotus franciscanus:*
Alaska to Baja. Shell diameters run to 6 ¼ in. (16 cm); the identifying long, primary spines measure up to 3 in. (8 cm). Red or red-brown in color, sometimes dark purple to black. The gonads are often eaten raw. Found in rocky kelp beds in the very low-intertidal zone to 295 ft. (90 m) on both protected and exposed shores.

Green sea urchin *Strongylocentrotus droebachiensis:*
Circumpolar, Alaska to California. This small urchin has a shell diameter to 3 $^1/_2$ in. (9 cm) with crowded, thin, short spines to 1 $^1/_5$ in. (3 cm) long. Pale green with dark tube feet; rarely a light purple in color. Found at the low-intertidal zone and subtidally on protected and exposed coasts.

Purple sea urchin *Strongylocentrotus purpuratus:*
Vancouver Island to Baja. This is a small urchin, with a shell of up to 4 in. (10 cm) in diameter; its short, stout, and blunt spines grow up to 1 $^1/_5$ in. (3 cm) long. Its color is typically bright purple, occasionally pale green or green-purple. Common in the low-intertidal zone and tidepools, often in holes or depressions worn in the rocks; in areas of moderate to strong wave action. Found to depths of 525 ft. (160 m).

Collection of sea urchins

The most common sea urchin and the target species of the commercial fishery is the red sea urchin, which is the largest urchin in the world. The green urchin is also abundant in many areas but is so small that processing is very difficult and the cost prohibitive.

The small purple urchin is often found in rocky tidepools on surf-beaten shores.

The giant red urchin and the green urchin are sometimes exposed at the lowest tides but are more easily harvested by skin or scuba diving. Be careful of the sharp spines!

Commercial fishing for red urchins usually takes place in the late fall and winter. Urchins are harvested by divers, who use a small rake-like tool to pick the urchins off the rocks and transfer them into bags.

52 Preparation of sea urchins

Each urchin has 5 pieces of "roe." One large red sea urchin will yield 2 servings, while the smaller purple and green urchins yield a single serving.

Cut out the bottom center, the mouth ("Aristotle's lantern"), then crack open the sea urchin with a large knife. Wash and gently shake the loose insides out. Using a tablespoon, carefully remove the gonads, or "roe," clinging to the sides of the shell. Place the gonads in a wire or plastic basket and immerse in clean water to rinse off the viscera and shell or spine fragments. Drain in a shallow basket or on absorbent paper towels. Protect from direct sunlight and keep cool.

Cooking of sea urchins

Sautéed sea urchin roe

> Sea urchin roe
> $^1/4$ cup (125 g) butter
> onion, finely chopped
> $^1/2$ tsp. (2.5 mL) lemon juice

Sauté some finely chopped onion in butter. Add lemon (or lime) juice, and then fry roe quickly, 30 seconds to 1 minute on each side.

Sea urchin butter

> 3 Tbsp. (45 mL) roe from one urchin
> $^1/4$ cup (125 g) butter

Cream softened butter and roe together and substitute this for butter in chowder and bisque recipes, or use as butter sauce for other seafoods such as clams or oysters.

Deviled or stuffed eggs with sea urchin roe

> 6 hardboiled eggs, cut in half lengthwise
> 2 Tbsp. (30 mL) butter
> 3 Tbsp. (45 mL) sea urchin roe (from one urchin)
> $^1/2$ tsp. (2.5 mL) lemon juice
> parsley, cut for garnish

Remove the egg yolks carefully. Blend with butter and roe until smooth. Add lemon ice. Stuff the egg whites with the mixture and garnish with parsley. Chill before erving.

One red sea urchin will yield enough roe to serve 2 persons, (5 pieces).

Red sea urchins can sometimes be collected at low tides.

Once you cut open the sea urchin, its edible gonads (roe) are easily removed.

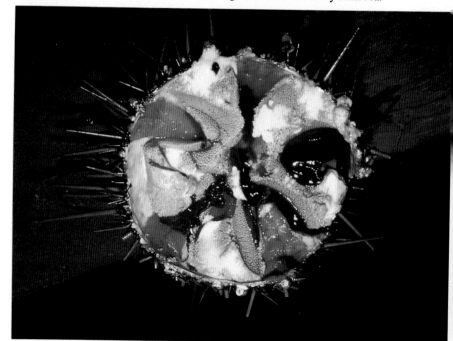

Marine Plants

Brown seaweeds

Bull kelp *Nereocystis leutkeana*:
This species grows subtidally, attached to rocks. It has a tubular stipe (like a stem) to 65 $^1/2$ ft. (20 m) long that ends at the surface with a bulb, and trailing blades to 10 ft. (3 m) long. The stipe can be cut and used for pickles. Forms extensive kelp beds along shores and reefs.

Kombu (refers to any of a number of brown kelps) *Laminaria saccharina, L. groenlandica, Alaria marginata, Cymathere triplicata.*
Laminaria saccharina is a rich brown color, with a smooth, thin, blade to 11 $^1/2$ ft. (3.5 m) long, with or without 2 rows of blister-like markings. It has a root-like holdfast and short stipe (stem). Found on rock in the lower-intertidal and subtidal zones. Take only small, young, and tender plants.

Seaweeds

Seaweeds have long been used in Oriental cookery, and many recipes can be four in Oriental and natural-food cookbooks. Seaweeds are commonly used as a dri supplement, added to soups, stews, casseroles, and salads. In the Orient, many speci of marine plants are cultured for human consumption. There is interest in Britis Columbia and Washington in growing kelp, or kombu, from local species *Laminar groenlandica* and *Cymathere triplicata*. Cultured plants can be selected for high quali and can be grown so that they are easy to harvest. Another local seaweed of grea potential is Nori, which is the dried, papery seaweed wrapped around fish and ric to make sushi. West Coast species of *Porphyra* may be suitable for culture for th North American sushi market.

In California there are great underwater forests of the giant kelp, *Macrocystis*, whic are harvested and processed to produce alginate. Alginate is used for texture an consistency in such common foods as ice cream and salad dressings. It is also used i the preparation of a wide variety of products including pharmaceuticals, paints, an paper products. Kelp is also regarded as a useful source of minerals, and kelp table are often available in grocery and drug stores.

NOTE: Do not collect exposed seaweeds at low tides; wade in or dive to take plants As with other seafoods, avoid areas where there may be pollutants.

Brown Seaweeds (see pictures, page 55)

Preparation of brown seaweeds

To dry seaweed, first wash in several changes of fresh water to remove any encrusting animals or plants. Then experiment with low, warming temperatures i the oven.

Cooking of brown seaweeds

Ham in dried seaweed

> ham strips, cut $^1/4$ in. by 2 in. long (0.6 by 5 cm)
> seaweed (nori or kombu), cut in strips to wrap ham

Soak sheets of dried seaweed in water, then wrap it around the ham strips. Bake ir a preheated oven at 350°F (180°C) until the seaweed is browned and crispy, 15 to 20 minutes. Seaweed for breakfast? Precook some sausages, wrap with seaweed, and bake.

Green seaweeds (see picture, page 58)

Uses:

Sea lettuce does not work for fresh salads, but can be dried and used in cooked dishes, substituted for or mixed with spinach or shredded cabbage. *Ulva* makes a good soup base and background flavor for clear soups.

(Continued)

Red seaweeds (see pictures, pages 58 & 59)

Red seaweeds that are edible include the many species of nori or laver, *Porphyra* , the "turkish towel," *Gigartina*, and dulse, *Rhodymenia*.

Preparation of red seaweeds

Nori is dried and processed into thin, paper-like sheets. It is available at specialty stores. You can experiment with drying local species at a warming temperature in the oven, in a dehydrator, or by hanging it to dry in the sun.

NOTE: Before drying, thoroughly wash the seaweed in several changes of fresh water to remove any encrusting animals or other plants.

Cooking of red seaweeds

Seaweed pudding

What better way to end this book than with a dessert recipe?

> 1 cup (250 mL) Turkish towel seaweed,
>   chopped and tied in a cheesecloth bag
> 1 quart (1 liter) milk
> 1 1/2 cups (375 mL) sugar (or honey)
> 1/4 tsp. (large pinch) of salt
> add any fruit for flavor (try 2 large apples, peeled, cored, and chopped)

Heat milk and the bag of seaweed in a double boiler for 30 minutes. Stir occasionally and press the bag for extracts from the seaweed. The milk will not thicken particularly. Remove and discard the bag. Add the sugar and salt, and allow to cool. As the pudding is cooling, add the fruit and pour into serving dishes. Chill for several hours to set.

Bon appetit!

Green Seaweed

Sea lettuce *Ulva species:*
Thin broad, lettuce-like blades to 16 in. (40 cm) long; yellow-green to dark green. Common in the intertidal zone, on rocks, and deeper.

Red Seaweed

Purple laver or nori *Porphyra spp.:*
Iridescent to purplish-black, with thin blades that are one cell thick. Blades are up to 20 in. (50 cm) long. They have an oily appearance when left dry on the rocks. Collect from the water at mid-tides.

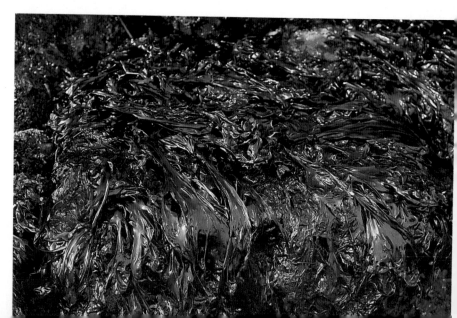

Turkish towel *Gigartina spp.:*
Wine-red to purplish-red in color, this species is characterized by numerous bumpy projections on the blades. Found in the mid- to low- intertidal zones.

Metric conversions

Canada has adopted the metric system in many areas, but the transition is not complete. The conversion of recipes to metric is not simple because of the difference of 5 to 10% in the common units of measure.

Metric cookery utensils are available in sets of 1, 2, 5, 15, and 25 mL spoons. Larger sets include 50 mL, 125 mL, 250 mL, 500 mL, and 1000 mL, which is one liter.

Approximate measurement equivalents:

(Rounded to conform with standard measuring utensils for cooking)

1 tsp. = 5 mL (is a little more than 1 tsp.)
1 Tbsp. = 15 mL

$^1/4$ cup = 4 Tbsp. = 60 mL
$^1/3$ cup = 75 mL
$^1/2$ cup = 125 mL
$^3/4$ cup = 180 mL
1 cup = 250 mL (is a little more than the 8-oz. cup)

1 fluid oz. = 30 mL
1 pint = 2 cups = 500 mL
1 quart = 2 pints = 4 cups = 1 liter (is a little more than the Imperial quart)

Mass—Weights: solid measures

1 ounce = 30 g (is a little more than 1 oz.)
$^1/4$ lb. = 4 oz. = 125 g
$^1/2$ lb. = 8 oz. = 250 g
$^3/4$ lb. = 12 oz. = 375 g
1 pound = 16 oz. = 500 g (is a little more than 1 lb.)
2.2 pounds = 1 kilogram (kg)

Temperatures:

FAHRENHEIT	CELCIUS	FAHRENHEIT	CELCIUS
5	-15	375	190
14	-10	400	200
32	0	425	220
50	10	450	230
200	100	500	260
300	150	525	270
325	160	550	290
350	180		

The challenge of catching coonstripe shrimp for dinner is half the fun.

Other conversion figures

(To convert, multiply the unit by the equivalent figure given here.
eg.: 3 in. = 3 x 2.54 = 7.62 cm.)

1 inch = 2.54 cm	1 cm = 0.3937 in.
1 foot = 0.3048 meters	1 m = 39.37 in. = 3.28 ft.
1 yard = 0.914 meters	
1 km = 0.621 mi.	1 statute mile = 1.609 kilometers

1 fathom = 6 feet = 1.83 meters

1 ounce = 28.57 g	1 g = 0.035 oz.
1 pound = 454 g = 0.45 kg	1 kg = 2.204 lb.
(rounded to 500 g)	

Everything inside the pink and spiny scallops can be eaten, or select out the round muscle.

Collecting gooseneck barnacles makes for an enjoyable outing. →

A diver's knife will make short work of shucking the rock scallop.

INDEX